Dr. King has been a pastor, mentor, and friend to me for nearly 20 years. God has gifted him with an unusual insight into healthy life and ministry practices. I've been a student of leadership principles for longer than I've been in ministry. This is one of the most practical resources I've encountered for leaders who are balancing the demands of life and ministry. Be careful, though. It's convicting!

—Dr. Jeff Philpott, Pastor, Sandhills Community Church, Columbia, S.C.
www.sandhillschurch.org

At Columbia International University we teach and model, as a community, both Sabbath rest and fruitful work. We even cancel classes once a month to have a day of prayer together. Yet, even with the support of the university's schedule and structure, it's very difficult to slow down. To help make the truth a reality, Roy has written an excellent how-to guide for all Christian workers (paid or volunteer) to discover and experience the joy of living by God's rhythm of time.

—Dr. Bill Jones, President, Columbia International University, Columbia, S.C.
www.ciu.edu

TIME MANAGEMENT IS REALLY LIFE MANAGEMENT

Roy King

Columbia, South Carolina

CONTENTS

7   Foreword by Robertson McQuilkin

9   Introduction

13   Chapter One – God's Perspective on Time

18   Chapter Two – A Dangerous Division of Time

24   Chapter Three – God's Perspective on Work Time

29   Chapter Four – God's Perspective on Rest Time

34   Chapter Five – Alignment of My Time

43   Study Guide

54   Notes

FOREWORD

I wish I had read this masterful treatment of time management at the beginning of my life, instead of at its end! Distilled from his ministry as consultant to hundreds of churches and ministries, refined by his own painful experience, and completed with research of the literature on time management, Roy King provides a realistic road map for navigating the demands of any life that seems to have an inadequate time allotment.

Who among us has not longed for the proverbial 36-hour day? Well, fret those time limitations no more. Help is in your hand!

My favorite chapters in this short treatise are the Sabbath or rest day analysis (chapter four) and the final chapter of step-by-step practical application of the principles laid out in earlier chapters. Roy's specialty in seminary classrooms and in his consulting ministry is the field of leadership. Here he extracts a central secret to effective leadership—managing one's daily, weekly, yearly calendar and the limited resources of any ministry, thriving or struggling.

Don't skip the earlier chapters which lay the foundation of biblical principles. And for maximum benefit, don't skip the suggested application exercises.

Enjoy this short, fun read, and find life-focus in the profound analysis of biblical truth about God's great gift of time.

Robertson McQuilkin
President Emeritus
Columbia International University

June 2009

I dedicate this book to those who are teaching me how to live:

To my wife, Pandora, who is my guide, helping me to see every person as a treasured gift from God.

To my daughter, Mary, who models for me how to grow by learning.

To my son, Mark, who teaches me to expect that creativity and wisdom will come as surprises when we play.

To my son-in-law, David, who helps me reach out to others in loving actions.

To my daughter-in-law, Jelayne, who inspires me by standing up for truth and sacrificing to love others.

WHY I HAD TO ATTEMPT THIS WRITING

I became a Christian in June 1972 at Explo' 72, a Campus Crusade Event held in Dallas, Texas. For one week, 85,000 high school and college students came together. It made the cover of *LIFE* magazine. It seemed that everywhere I went after that, I would run into folks who had attended or who were influenced by a friend whose spiritual journey had been impacted by the conference.

Within the next year, God moved me into leadership of our Campus Crusade ministry at East Tennessee State University and I served a church as part-time youth pastor. When I graduated in 1975, I went on staff with Campus Crusade. Since then I have served in a variety of ministry leadership roles ranging from administration at Columbia International University, to pastoral staff, senior pastor and seminary professor.

Between 1977 and 1995 I had three crashes. I have used a variety of expressions—"hitting the wall", "burn out", "stress-induced depression"— to attempt to define what occurred in my emotional and physical life during those times. The way God brought me through each of those seasons involved my wife standing beside me in compassionate support, and special friends who did not judge me, but who cared enough to confront me when I was blinded by my own destructive emotions. Three different counselors provided perspective and asked good questions as I struggled to find my way out of the pain.

During these times I wanted to quit ministry and even life. I thirsted for anything that promised a quick relief to my pain. The people God intended me to serve became people that I did not care about, and whose requests and needs triggered anger and resentment. Every contact was one more voice wanting a piece of me. I developed intense stomach problems and extreme fatigue. I gained weight. I would swing between frantic and non-stop work, and the inability to get out of bed and do simple things.

I could fill several books with the lessons that God taught me during those months of struggle interspersed among more than 18 years of parachurch and church leadership experience. But one common theme that began to emerge was how I made my daily and weekly choices in using the time God gave me. My journey became a healing path as I slowly changed the rhythm of my life to align with God's design for how I am made to live. To use biblical terms, repentance in this area of my life involved changing how I spent my time, and the fruit of that change has been a drastic increase in satisfaction with my life and a more healthy state of living.

So, I write not out of strength in the skills of time management but as one who had to change and grow in this area to survive. I write out of weakness that God has mercifully filled with his strength.[1]

I feel that I must write as a witness. I must tell of my discovery of life as God intended when we align our use of time with God's perspective.

Since the mid-90s, God has allowed me to supervise, teach and coach other leaders. Youth pastors, pastors, counselors, CEOs and missionaries are just a few of the hats these men and women are wearing. Many of them were drawn to me as I began sharing my struggles and what God was teaching me.

In this book I have organized some of the lessons from my journey. I have mentioned some books and passages of the Bible that were fresh, cool water to my parched and weary heart. I have sought to be biblically-based so that these lessons can be applied in any cultural context, and to be very practical so that leaders can emerge with clear actions they can live out.

Many of my seminary students and leaders that I coach come to me with areas of leadership and disciple-making they want to improve:

1. *I need help developing a team of leaders who can lead with me.*
2. *I need to be less consumed by church or mission "machinery" and spend more significant time in evangelism and basic disciple-making.*
3. *My spouse says I am not investing in our home and parenting as I should.*
4. *I do not have any friendships that go beyond my leadership role. I am close to my elders and some other core leaders but our lives only intersect at the ministry level. If I were no longer the pastor, we would have no other connection.*
5. *I am angry, and filled with too much lust, greed, and other dark stuff.*

I have observed that if I jump to a diagnosis and recommend changes addressing these concerns, it often comes across as adding more items to an already jammed schedule. The leader may agree with my observations and suggestions about needed changes, but often feels powerless, trapped in a storm of activity that leaves very little margin for making adjustments. It's like being in a hurricane, with no electricity, no running water, and no way to travel—and a friend shows up and suggests that the solution is to go shopping and prepare a nice big meal (imagine the perfect Thanksgiving dinner). The prescription, while attractive, and even desired, is simply not a reasonable course of action.

One primary difference between being in a hurricane and a ministry worker's daily lifestyle is that we have more options than we realize. We can either focus on the choices within our circle of responsibility, or we can continue to feed the idea that we are overwhelmed by the storms of circumstance, powerless before a flood of expectations, and left with only one option—complaining.

I believe that a leader changing his or her perspective on time is foundational to being able to make other changes. It requires going back to the very basics. There is a story told of Vince Lombardi, the famous coach, holding up a football to his players and saying, "This is a football." In a similar way, God is holding up our calendars and saying, "This is time." My desire is for us to hold up our Bibles, especially the first three chapters of Genesis, and to ask one simple question: "God, how do you view this thing you have created that we call time?" Applying his answer makes the difference between living life as he intended and oscillating between feelings of bondage and boredom.

To assist you in making changes in your use of your time, there is a study guide at the end of the five chapters. I suggest you stop at the end of each chapter to complete the questions and activities in the study guide.

It will also help you to make lifestyle changes that stick if you process these lessons with someone who has traveled or is traveling some of this same challenging journey regarding time and life management.

CHAPTER 1

HOW GOD VIEWS OUR TIME

Objectives:

To clearly understand the ways God divides our time.

To make a commitment to learn from the past, to lean into the future and to live in the present.

Dr. Bobby Clinton says leadership is about *perspective.* The better the leader's perspective is, the greater the potential for effective leadership. A gift God often gives leaders is the ability to see things that most other people do not yet see. This does not make leaders better than anyone else, but this way of looking at what is going on is a very valuable gift to those under their leadership.

I train leaders to develop a spiritual habit of asking God to let them see as he sees. As they view people, circumstances and structures within their horizon, they seek a divine perspective. They see problems realistically, but also as opportunities for growing in faith. They truly feel the pain and cost of a course of action, but press on with the journey with God-centered hope. They do not back down or let those around them drift away from loving even their enemies.

The goal is for leaders in God's service to deeply desire to see every element of life as God sees it, and to hunger for the functional authority guiding their choices to come from God as he has revealed himself in creation[2] and in the Bible[3]. So in this chapter let's consider God's perspective on our time.

Time is a precious resource, a gift entrusted to us by God. We have no idea how much of it he will give to us. We shout with Job, "God gives and God takes away, but blessed be the name of our Lord."[4] Unlike money—which can be spent, earned, lost or found—time is like sand leaking from a bag as we walk along. It only goes one way, and can never be re-collected.

Because time is a series of moments that we can never recover or do over, it is the most critical resource we have in our possession. In science fiction, the ability to move around in time by visiting the past or making changes in the future has been a part of many attractive story lines. Perhaps this denial of the rules of time is compelling because we feel so locked up within its boundaries. There is something in our hearts that wants to break free and live beyond the constraints of time. We long to control time, instead of letting it dictate the course of our lives. This may be part of what the biblical writer meant by "God placing eternity in our hearts."[5]

Consider several of the ways that God divides up time:

1. God divides time into the past, the present and the future.

God has created us to live within a specific moment of time we call the present. Part of God making us in his image is that we possess the capacity to choose. But we can only choose in the present. People rightly sense that present circumstances flow from past choices and set the stage for future options. But in reality the only place in time where we can choose is in the present moment.

God's boundaries on time cause us to view time in terms of past, present and future. We can be creative, make investments, and watch as time moves the present into the past. We can learn from our past. God commands us in many places to "remember" the past and learn from those memories.[6] We are to live differently in the present because of our reflection on the past. Mining lessons from our past experience is part of the journey to wisdom.

We access God's grace and truth as we remember. Baptism and communion are two common ways the church remembers. We do not live in the past, but we are to learn from it, letting God's past actions strengthen our present faith. "To remember is, literally, to put broken pieces back together, to re-member. It is to create an original wholeness out of what have been scattered fragments … There is a terrible cost to our busyness. It erodes memory."[7]

We can also advance into the future with plans and hope anchored in God's promises. In the church we talk about our "blessed hope," as we look for and eagerly await the return of Christ. Our vision of a future of living in his coming kingdom should color our present choices just as much as lessons learned from our past. We live to lay up treasures in heaven and see ourselves as "pilgrims" or "aliens" passing through this world. We live with a sense of anticipation and a longing for glory, for we are on a journey with an eternal home as our destination. Because of our hope of a future destination, our present choices are made differently from those who live simply for fulfillment in the present.

So, we learn from the past but cannot go back and choose it to be different. And as we look ahead we anticipate a future of glory, perfection and God's kingdom in full exposure. Future hope influences our priorities in the present, but we cannot control the future. Our plans are like writing with our finger in the dust and God does not grant us the power to force them into reality. God does not give us control over the future. The future is hidden in the hand of our sovereign God who will walk with us into it, but chooses to not give us details in advance. The past and the future are sandboxes reserved for our Creator's play. We look into them but cannot live in them.

We should see opportunities that lie in the future but avoid the "greener pasture" mindset. We must be very careful of statements like, "When we get (fill in the blank with what you need) we will be able to…" as if the resources of the present are not enough for today's obedience. The best way to advance into the future in faith may be our gratitude and celebrations for God's provision in the present.

God has assigned us to the present. We love or hate in the present. We trust or fear in the present. We give or take in the present. Our choices in the present shape and reveal the motives of our heart.

The most important choices we make are the hundreds of small commitments in how we will invest each present moment as it arrives. We must:

Be Fully Present.
Be Fully Devoted.
Be Fully Surrendered.

2. *God divides time into days and seasons.*

From the creation accounts (Genesis 1–2, and John 1) we understand that God also divides time into day and night as well as seasons of sowing, growth, harvest and death. Even in parts of the world where they do not have four defined seasons, there is still a rhythm of rainy and dry seasons. Many of God's gifts are supplied one day or season at a time. I cannot sleep once and then be done with it. I cannot eat once and then out grow my need for it. God has designed us to daily receive what we need from his hand.

3. *The most significant way God divides time is the weekly rhythm.*

Six days for work and one day for rest is very important to God. He ordered his own creative acts around that rhythm of producing and rest. Notice that he created a day for rest before sin entered into the creation through Adam and Eve's rebellion (Genesis 2:1–3). In what we often call the Ten Commandments in Exodus 20, God features rest as part of his will for us. He gives the same priority to stopping work one day out of seven as he does to not killing or committing adultery. The law was given as a gift from God to his lost children to help them discern his design and blueprint. God's ten laws describe the choices we are to make as we live in our present moments. They reflect his design for how he made us to live at our best.

There are some lessons God wants to teach us that can only be learned when we choose to rest. Work is good, of course, and we will spend two chapters of this book looking at God's perspective on our work. But rest is also God's gracious gift to us. As Jesus said, "The Sabbath was made for man, not man for the Sabbath" (Mark 2:27).

Imagine that you gave me a very costly, beautifully-wrapped gift with a warm hug and a whisper in my ear assuring me that it was given just because you are very fond of me. How would you feel if I replied, "Thank you for the gift," but then tossed it into the back corner of a closet? What would you think of how I view your gift if I said, "It is August and things are very busy. I will take a break the day after Christmas and I will come find your present in the back of the closet and open it then"?

God designed you and created time for you to live in. Your dwelling place is called the present, or "this" day. To live well in your present moments, God gives you a day of rest to enjoy every seventh day. In chapter two, we will examine some dangerous ways of viewing time. This is foundational to our later exploration of work days (chapter three) and rest days (chapter four). We will conclude with practical steps for living in a work and rest rhythm (chapter five).

CHAPTER 2

A DANGEROUS DIVISION OF TIME

Objectives:

To repent of dividing time as secular and sacred.

*To make a clear commitment of acknowledging all
of my time as a gift from God.*

Many Christians are taught that Christ-followers should give some of their money to support what God is doing through the church. Some are taught that disciples are expected to give at least a tithe of their income to their church, often defined as ten percent. Offerings are defined in some church traditions as financial gifts made above the tithe. In those contexts, giving money is called bringing the tithes and offerings. Some churches do not teach tithe and offering giving, but they will still challenge God's people to give as a joyful act of obedience.

Even with these different definitions of giving, most Christian leaders would agree that the reason for giving is to say from one's heart to God:

"Everything I have I have received from you. Giving a portion of it to the church is my way of honoring you, thanking you and reminding myself that it all belongs to you. Give me your wisdom to use all of what you give me for your glory."

If instead, a Christian says, *"God, here is your part and what is left is mine to do with as I desire,"* this attitude would likely indicate immaturity and perhaps a rebellious or hypocritical spirit. For a Christian, to declare Jesus as King and Lord surely includes his lordship over wealth and possessions.

What is true of our financial resources is also true of our time. Yet in many cultures, including the American church culture, time is often divided into small boxes we label *secular* and *sacred*. There is great danger in holding to this perspective of our time.

Here are a few incorrect perspectives about time:

1. God only works in sacred time.

If I believe this, I tend to assume that Sunday messages or other activities in my "sacred" box are the only means God uses to touch my life. I will fail to see how waiting in traffic or in a check-out line can be the practice of a spiritual discipline that allows God to grow patience within me.

2. God only cares about sacred time.

This leads to paying God off with a few hours a week of church or spiritual activities and then ignoring his vision for how the rest of my time is invested. It leads to a subtle distance from God. My relationship with Christ fails to influence all of my choices and responses. This is the birthplace of hypocrisy.

3. God wants to be in first place on my priority list.

I meet many Christians who have been taught to set up a list of priorities that goes something like this:

1. God
2. Family
3. Work
4. Church
5. Community
6. Self

There are many variations on this list but the big point to understand is that this is not biblical. Instead, the Bible describes disciples as having responsibilities in *all* of these relationships and each relationship is a gift from Christ. Every relationship includes responsibilities that are opportunities for acts of obedience energized and motivated from a heart of faith, hope and love.

The priority list fails to be an effective tool for making decisions. If these boxes really exist, where do we put something like prayer? Most people would put it in the "God" box. But in reality, we are to be praying about everything and all of the time![8]

If caring for self is always the lowest priority in the list, it may explain why we have many Christ-followers who are depressed, fatigued, and out-of-shape physically and mentally. In reality, God created us as complex beings and He has a design for our choices that includes all aspects of our self:

- Physical
- Mental
- Emotional
- Spiritual
- Social

Notice that this is not a numbered priority list. If we ignore God's blueprint for any of these aspects, our individual health is affected. Our physical body is a temple in which God dwells. We are members of the body of Christ. To ignore our need for rest and to fail to practice principles of health dishonors the name of Christ that is now part of our identity.

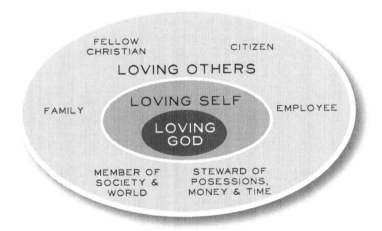

God assigns, or blesses us, with a variety of roles and responsibilities. Think of them as "hats" that he gives us to wear as we move through our days. I have a husband hat as well as son, employee, brother, friend, parent, citizen and child-of-God hats. In the Bible, God provides clarity on the responsibilities that go with each relationship. And if I am having difficulty locating the biblical teaching for a specific role, he has provided a summary that is the "bottom line" for every relationship and role I am given.

Think of life this way: Every person lives as if inside two circles. The inner circle is a circle of responsibility. Everything can either occur or not occur based on my choices. What God assigns as my responsibility can only be blocked by my choice. I stand alone before God to answer for how I fulfilled it. I can't be responsible for a good marriage; that takes two of us. But I am responsible to be a good spouse. I can't be responsible for my aging parents being happy or content, but I can be responsible to be a good son.

There is a dramatic difference on how I view my accountability to God. God says, "Roy, you are responsible *for*... (that is my circle of responsibility). And you are responsible *to*... (that is my circle of influence).

The outer circle is a circle of influence God gives me—contributions to make to others. My influence can occur by praying, encouraging, teaching and a hundred other ways. Choices in my circle of influence contribute to what God is doing in others' lives. For example, I am responsible to put these words on the page and if I watch TV instead, it will not happen. My choice blocks or carries out my responsibility. But if I do write these words, I pray these words will influence others, though I am not responsible for that outcome.

Dr. Bill Bright, founder of Campus Crusade for Christ, defined being a witness as "sharing Christ in the power of the Holy Spirit and leaving the results up to God." I believe that definition holds true for any area of obedience. A person who needs a job looks for a job in the power of the Holy Spirit and leaves the results up to God. One of my favorite preachers, Ron Dunn, now in heaven, said, "The problem in the Christian life is that we are always trying to do things only God can do and refuse to do the things God has told us to do." Does that make you look at your "to do" list in a different way?

"... you shall love the Lord your God with all your heart and with all your soul and with all of your mind and with all your strength.' ... 'You shall love your neighbor as yourself.' There is no other commandment greater than these."

— *Mark 12:30-31* ESV

All of my choices are shaped by one big question—*How do I love God and the neighbors who are in my circle of relationship in this moment?* (Romans 13:8–10). Clarifying who and what I am responsible *for* and responsible *to* helps me define how to love a person. I do not love well if I am trying to be responsible for the other person's choices. They end up feeling controlled, smothered or manipulated.

Since we are made in his image and he is *love*, it follows that this would be the center of the target for the choices we make. Jesus demonstrated the love that God has for every person. His love took the form of a great sacrifice that was done willingly and even joyfully for the sake of every person. He also knew what the ones being loved needed and he gave exactly what was needed—sin-cleansing reconciliation that moved us from eternal death to eternal life. But notice Christ never *forced* anyone to follow him. He never violated their circle of responsibility.

I recently heard a student life dean describe parents of college students as "helicopter parents." They hover over their kids, expecting continual cell phone updates. In our culture it seems parenting gravitates toward extremes. Either we ignore our children and leave them to raise themselves (ignoring our God-assigned responsibility *to* influence) or we try to control them (to be responsible *for* their actions).

To get more specific, we need to think about a definition for the love that God calls us to choose. I propose this definition:

I love when I joyfully sacrifice in order to give what is really needed for the sake of the beloved.

Using these two circles helps us define loving without crossing the line and violating the other person's God-created capacities as a thinking, feeling, and choosing being who is responsible to God.

Once we see every moment as a gift coming from God it also becomes more real to us that God is with us in each moment. God does not wait in the sacred box for us to show up at the sacred times.

In this chapter we confronted two wrong concepts about time:

1. *That there is sacred time and secular time.*

2. *That our priority is God first, family second, work third, and self last.*

When we replace these with God's perspective, we find ourselves living every moment in God's presence, and we see how we live in a web of relationships where we love God and others as we love ourselves.

In chapter three, we will examine a biblical view of our responsibility to pursue fruitful work.

CHAPTER 3

GOD'S PERSPECTIVE ON WORK TIME

Objectives:

To gain clarity on the stages of work from sowing seed to reaping the harvest.

To expect resistance to our work and strategies for responding to it.

God made us to bear fruit! We have an inner desire for our lives to count. We want to make a difference, contribute, or leave a legacy. This inner goal is rooted in our basic design for productive work, flowing from being made in the image of a working Creator. As I walked outside early this morning and saw the stars shining brightly in a clear sky, I shouted out, "God you sure do good work!"

There are cultural differences in defining productivity. Being fruitful in some cultures is equated to tasks accomplished while in others it is in life-giving relationship. Some cultures promote individual effort while some promote community accomplishments. What is a basic biblical perspective on our work time that affirms or corrects our cultural perspective?

In chapter one, we listed some of the ways time is divided, including the agricultural rhythm that flows with the seasons. God created the world in such a way that most of what is produced is transformed from seed to fruit. This biological progression was a common experience of Adam's original work as he tended the garden (Genesis 2:15). After Adam and Eve rebelled against God's rule (Genesis 3), God increased the resistance that would accompany Adam's work. God did not remove the desire for productive work but he did design hurdles to fruitfulness: "In pain you shall eat of it all of the days of your life" (Genesis 3:17). Work itself is not the result of disobeying God, but the resistance to our efforts at being fruitful is intended by God.

Consider the elements of the agricultural work cycle:

1. Sowing
2. Nurturing
3. Protecting
4. Harvesting

Sowing – Scattering the seed. The farmer breaks up the soil so the seed can be easily buried. In a mysterious way, there in the damp darkness, God has placed life in the seed that breaks out and grows.

[handwritten: Getting ideas / Praying / Talking to others / Spreading passion.]

Nurturing – God must provide the right amount of sun, rain and food for the growing plant to survive. The farmer can often contribute some supplemental water or fertilizer but in most cases the survival of the plants depends on God giving the essential contribution.

[handwritten: Setting up leadership. / Pray for specific / Getting locations / literate / contacts]

Protecting – There is opposition to growth. Bugs attack. Birds, rabbits and other animals make a meal out of the tender plant. Blight and disease can kill or damage the plant. Weeds threaten to choke it out. The good farmer invests the sweat to fight them all.

[handwritten: Pray for protection / Encourage leaders / Solve problems.]

Harvesting – Now comes the fruit. Often months of labor go by with very little fruit. Buds turn into blooms which then grow into the fruit which then slowly ripens. And at just the right moment, in a flurry of depleting around the clock investment of energy, the harvest is gathered before it spoils in the field.

[handwritten: Aug, 15 – leaving leadership in place]

Genesis 3 also broadens this understanding of fruitfulness to the woman having a child. The seasons of conception, pregnancy, labor and delivery share many similar elements to farming a crop.

These same four stages are present in the birth of a business, the birth of a new ministry or almost any productive work we attempt. They may not be quite as sequential as the biological journey from seed to fruit but the season of work required is often a guide to decision-making.

Psalm 126:5-6 describes the agony of sowing and the joy of harvesting as a metaphor for the work of God. In Psalm 127:3, children are seen as the fruit of a family built by God. Psalm 107:34-38 portrays a beautiful image of our all-powerful God who is ultimately responsible for the waste or fruitfulness of the work of people. Jesus continues the idea of fruitfulness through his parables, his encounters with the Samaritans (including a woman at the well), and his teaching on being the vine who blesses his branches with fruit. Paul also speaks of God assigning some people to sowing and others to harvesting (1 Corinthians 3:1-5). Growth and bearing fruit are viewed as essential parts of a new life in God (Colossians 1:6, 10). In Paul's last letter, 2 Timothy, he parallels the ministry of making disciples to the labor of a hardworking farmer. To view any fruitful labor as going through stages from seed to harvest is a common biblical perspective.

Sowing – We cast many ideas around. We brainstorm broadly. We "blue sky" think, pray, and trust that from many of our creative thoughts at least a few will take root and begin to grow into a solution to a problem, an answer to a need, or a victory to a challenge in our work.

Nurturing – Most new work goes through a season of fragile establishment. We do our best to invest what has been entrusted to us but we know that if God doesn't supply passionate leaders, finances, or other resources that are beyond our capacity, the start-up may die out.

Protecting – There are corruptions that can grow from within and there are enemies that may attack from the outside. Work always takes place on battlefields, or other places of resistance. It is an odd truth that the world needs the seed-to-fruit cycle to survive and yet the threats are often so great that fruitfulness seems impossible. It is miraculous that God gets anything done in the church with the combination of sinful workers with whom he ties his activity, and the resistance that he allows. Satan throws up hindrances, but God provides ways around and through (1 Thessalonians 2:18, 3:2).

Harvesting – Nothing beats the juicy reward of ripe fruit. There is nothing like the "light bulb" of a student's understanding coming on as a reward to the teacher patiently sowing and working with students. There is nothing like sharing in the joy of a new Christian freshly liberated from the burdens of guilt. As Paul describes the work of ministry in 1 Corinthians 3 , one plants and another waters but God gives the growth. In John 4, Jesus reminds the disciples of the joy of the sower and the reaper in God's harvest of souls.

How does the cycle of productive labor apply to our life management?

1.   **Work is really about being *productive* or *fruitful*.** Work is rarely satisfying if we sense we are just moving paper around on our desk. Work has a goal, a destination, a harvest which motivates vision and energizes hope. We may need to stop our work in order to clarify the goal, outcome or desired results. Lack of clarity paralyzes decision-making and leaves us feeling like we are wandering in an endless maze.

2.   **Work will always encounter resistance.** When we engage in productive labor, we frequently face the reality that our resources will not be enough. Humility is living in the reality that we need help. That help must come from outside of ourselves. Unless God helps us, little lasting impact will be accomplished. Resistance reminds us that our resources are never enough. The discipline that God planted into creation in Genesis 3 serves a very valuable purpose: it drives us to God. The confidence that we were designed to bear fruit is tempered with the awareness that we are inadequate to produce it by ourselves.

3.   **Fruitfulness is a mystery.** There is a part of seeing seed grow into a fruitful plant that we can understand and participate in—but God gives the growth, as Paul says three times in one short paragraph (1 Corinthians 3:5-9). That is why prayer is so foundational and essential in all of our work. It also limits our planning and control. Farmers, doctors and other specialists all want to research and understand the mystery of the seed, the new business, or the church plant, but there are limits to our ability to predict the perfect formula that will guarantee the intended result. If you question this, just go pull some

business books written ten years ago off the shelf and see what a short shelf life the perspective has contributed.

4.   **Work takes time.** A good farmer is a <u>patient farmer</u>. Shortcuts, fads, and miracle cures abound, designed to speed up and reduce the effort in losing weight, getting rich, growing a church or doing almost anything. They are of little value and in most cases are a distraction to the work that is really needed. Save your money! There is no $19.95 quick fix to accomplishing our work. Work requires sustained effort over time. Work is exerting the right kind of effort that suits each stage of the journey from seed to fruit. There is no short-cut.

5.   **Work demands discernment to know what kind of effort is needed at the right time.** A good farmer understands the seasons and gives the right kind of investment at the right time. If he pulls up weeds at the wrong time, he damages the plant growing nearby. If he waters at the wrong time, the plant rots. If he harvests too early, the fruit never ripens. If he prunes at the wrong time, he may miss a whole cycle of harvest or even kill the plant. If he sows at the wrong time, the plant may never break ground before it is killed in a harsh cold. Talk with an experienced church planter and you will see that these principles apply to more than just raising corn.

In chapter two, we looked at the danger of dividing time into sacred and secular categories. A similar misconception is that work is limited to what we are employed to do. Many of us work at a job for pay. Some of us also engage in a volunteer commitment of service in ministry. But parenting is also work. Marriage is work. Keeping up a house, automobile or other investments is work.

From God's perspective, work is any productive, fruitful effort, assigned to us by God, for us to labor at six days each week.

Anyone who works hard looks forward to rest. In chapter four, we will look at a biblical perspective on rest as a beautiful gift from God to his creation.

CHAPTER 4

GOD'S PERSPECTIVE ON REST TIME

Objective:

To clearly understand God's gift of rest and to
begin to practice weekly biblical rest.

"Sabbath is both a day and an attitude to nurture stillness."
— *Mark Buchanan,* The Rest of God

We leak! We all expend strength, vitality, and focus as we work. Depletion is a gift from God to set limits for our lives. We bear the image of our Creator but we do not share his unlimited power and strength. God does not leak. We do. Some of us have been taught it is noble to be in a continual place of exhaustion from our service to God. That implies we are in danger of being more spiritual than God who prescribed rest!

One of the reasons for the limit is found in Genesis 3 where God chose to block us from the tree of life. God did not want us to have the ability to live forever apart from him. Every time I am tired, I am being reminded that I am running down and my fatigue entices me to run to God for new life. Aging is another aspect of this same limit.

We leak and this means we require a frequent infusion of what is needed to live. We can't generate it from within ourselves; it must come from outside of us. We must take in food, water, air and everything else required for life. We even need to receive love from outside of ourselves to be alive as God intended. God intends for us to choose rest so that he can pour what is essential for life into us.

Let me say it again. No matter how young and virile you seem, you are leaking life. Your work, and the resistance encountered as you seek to be productive and fruitful, are always draining you. You must replenish, refresh, restore and rebuild. **And this life you need must come from outside of yourself.**

Rest is God's gift to you to replace what work takes out. One day of rest can replenish what six days of work takes out. In addition, God gave other work breaks to his people in the Bible called feasts and fasts. In some ways we have carried these breaks over into our experience today as retreats, holidays and vacations. God provides these rest places where we go to be replenished. Rest is a space that God gives us where we are removed from the expectations to be productive. "We grow at all levels by expending energy beyond our ordinary limits and then recovering."[9]

God gives you permission to rest one day out of seven and you should never feel guilty about it.

There are some things that God wants to teach you that you can only learn when you are resting. You can only really learn grace when you are at rest. You can only experience the reality of God loving you just as much when you are intentionally non-productive as when you are "useful." Trusting God to provide for and sustain the investment made during your working hours as you go "off the clock" can only be learned when you are resting.

In the previous chapter, we learned how work is used to replace pride with humility. Rest also develops humility. To stop working in order to give myself fully to rest affirms that I am not indispensable to God's activity in this world. Fruitful work is filled with the joy of harvest and non-productive rest is also a joy and peace, a refreshing drink of freedom.

If we try going several day-and-night cycles without sleep, our bodies very quickly start sending messages that all is not well. We cannot live for long by ignoring our daily work and rest rhythm. What messages are our bodies and souls sending us if we ignore God's weekly rhythm for Sabbath which he also created? Maybe it would be easier to Sabbath if God turned out the lights every seventh day!

What is rest? Resting is not the absence of intentional action; it is just intentionally choosing things like:

- Physically resting by taking a nap or listening to good music
- Delighting in small things—taking 30 minutes to watch a sunset
- Celebrating and meditating on great truths, such as the reality of our caring Father, the saving Son and the gracing Spirit

Not working may be pictured as childlike play, in the best sense. Playing has no goal to achieve, or end to accomplish, but the play itself is the end. Enjoy a playground swing. Draw in the sand. Listen to music and maybe even dance to it! Eat slowly, taking time to taste it and share it in the company of special friends. Wrestle with your dog. Take a long walk and talk out loud with God. Don't necessarily ask for things you need; just be with him, thanking and praising him. Biblical rest and childlike play look very similar.

Psalm 92 is called the Sabbath Psalm. Read it slowly out loud.
Now read it again.

Notice how the Psalmist speaks of how good the present moment is as he is refreshed. But also notice his visits into the past and the future. He remembers by reflecting on what God has done. He also refocuses his vision for the goal of his life. He paints a picture of the future—a fruitful living tree is his image for what he wants to become. Notice that the singer affirms God's presence in the past, present and future moments of life.

When I have tasted God's gift of resting, those three elements are often present. I am refreshed for the coming week. I am at a place of peaceful trust that comes from reflecting (for me that often includes writing in a journal), and I close my Sabbath by refocusing on the long term-vision of what God has for me (this often involves looking at my plans for the upcoming week and even a few weeks ahead to see if my plans align with his vision for me).

When I choose to say "yes" to too many things, they become the weight that presses me into a certain kind of person in the course of days, weeks and months. When I am rested, I see clearly where I need to make some changes in my time investments.

My son had this quote over his desk during his college days. Read it slowly and pause to reflect on what motivates your choices.

> *This is the beginning of a new day.*
> *God has given me this day to use as I will.*
> *I can waste it or use it for good,*
> *But what I do today is important*
> *Because I am investing a day of my life for it.*
> *When tomorrow comes, this day will be gone forever,*
> *Leaving in its place something I have traded for it.*
> *I want it to be gain and not loss, good and not evil,*
> *Success and not failure,*
> *In order that I shall not regret the price I have paid for it.*
> — *Anonymous*

Where do you begin?

First, you have to value a day of rest. What you really consider of high value gets your attention and intention. Do you see Sabbath the way God sees it? Do your values align with his?

Second, refuse to water down your day of rest. The reason I placed the lesson on work before the lesson on rest is because for many years I was trying to enter the gift of God's rest but very often failed to experience what I sensed the Bible was describing. My mistake was that I had made my definition of work too small. I was taking a day of rest from my paid job but diluted my day of rest with all of my other work responsibilities. I let working around the home and many other types of productive labor eat the heart out of my days of rest.

It has helped tremendously to schedule all work to end by 6:00 p.m. and then rest until 6:00 p.m. the next day. Pastor Pete Scazzero[10] of New Life Fellowship has been a mentor in my life in framing Sabbath around these hours. For those who have jobs at the church Pete suggests Sabbath from 6 p.m. Friday to 6 p.m. Saturday. For those who work a Monday through Friday job, Sabbath may be best for 6 p.m. Saturday through 6 p.m. Sunday. This may mean examining some of what churches often program on Sundays to see if it is really helping people enter into Sabbath, or if it is fruitful work that increases our depletion and dilutes our rest. If your job is in a field like emergency services where you work changing shifts and days, you may have to vary your rest times to accomodate your work schedule.

Third, recognize that you will be swimming against the current of your culture. The driven Western culture and many of our church cultures place very little value on rest. But disciples are called to display the Jesus culture. His followers are willing to let his definitions, expectations, and rhythm of living trump our cultural perspective. Disciples of Jesus who choose to live out his values will always be counter-cultural.

When I visited New Life Fellowship, Pete shared with me the negative reaction he initially received from the Asian students hearing him preach on Sabbath. They told him they simply could not perform to expected academics if they took a day off from their studies. Pete challenged them to test God for a few weeks and see what happened. They are now believers in the necessity of Sabbath! God's rhythm exposes our fear of failure and our prideful carrying of responsibility that only God is strong enough to handle. Something breaks inside of us when we lay the world off of our shoulders for even one day. It becomes easier to trust God as King on the other six days.

People who are not Christ-followers should see something so refreshingly different and alive about our lives that the Spirit can use to make them thirsty for God's grace and truth. Be prepared to be misunderstood when you begin saying, "No!" and set boundaries in your life to establish the work/rest rhythm. But know that the witness of a life in rhythm will make the new life in Christ visible and attractive.

So, how do you take your calendar and start to obey God in your work and rest days? Chapter five will help you get started.

CHAPTER 5

ALIGNMENT OF MY TIME

Objective:

*Gain practical assistance in developing a personal growth plan
for living a healthy rhythm with your time.*

*"I submit as Sabbath's golden rule: Cease from what is necessary.
Embrace that which gives life. And then do whatever you want."*
— *Mark Buchanan,* The Rest of God

Remember from our earlier lessons that we are defining work as any productive labor; not just our job. Work produces fruit. Rest is to stop working. Rest is being non-productive before God. Rest is the childlike, playful exploration of the gift of life. Like a hand in a glove, rest and work go together so that we experience the truly abundant life that God delights in providing for his children.

What are some of the benefits of weekly cycle of work and rest?

It helps me see all of my time as a gift from a good God. I have been married since 1976 and love my wife, Pandora, more now than when I proposed. One way this shows up is how I feel when I travel without her. It is very hard to see new sights and visit places of interest when I know that she would enjoy being there as well. My enjoyment goes down because at some level I am grieving not being able to share these moments with her.

Our God deeply loves us and is committed to walking through every moment with us. It must grieve him, or maybe that is what the Bible means by quenching the Spirit, when I do not acknowledge that he is present in all of my time.

When I return to work from my rest I have a better perspective. A rested person tends to see life differently. Other people working around me have commented on the fruit of wisdom, priority, clarity, compassion, discernment and creativity that seem to be present in greater quantity and quality when I am rested. When I am personally depleted, I tend to see all resources as scarce. I revert to protecting my shrinking energy level by simply getting work off my desk. Mistakes often occur when I am working from a place of fatigue, such as leaving people out who need to be included in the decision-making process.

One of the greatest resources we have to solve problems and make good decisions is creativity. To be creative is part of our being made in the image of our Creator. Creativity grows from being focused in our work and replenished from our rest. Creative expression expends a great deal of our energy and will drive us back to the place of renewal.

What are some basic practices that support a healthy work/rest cycle?

1.   Decide what matters.

One of my mentors, Robertson McQuilkin, tells me he prays that I will learn the 15th and 16th letters of the alphabet. He believes I need to say, "NO!" to more good things so I can invest myself in the work that really matters.

Pruning is very challenging and threatening. In my church consulting, the average congregation I serve needs to prune at least one third of their programs so they will have the energy, leadership capacity and other resources needed to really be involved in reaching out. Christians, and entire churches, easily drift into the consumer mentality of a "cruise ship" style of ministry when what is needed is the clarity and commitment of a battleship crew accomplishing a mission. Cruise ships pride themselves on overwhelming those choosing to sail with them with nonstop activity to fulfill any whim. On a battleship, every person on the crew and every item on board is justified in light of fulfilling its next mission. We must frequently revisit what outcomes we are intending and then ask what seeds would have to be sown to reap that result.

For example: If our church desires to start other churches, what specific prayers need to be answered, and what specific investments need to be made right now—in the present moment God has given us—that move us toward that outcome? And what do we need to abandon, and how do we prune it without unduly hurting others, in order to focus on what we believe to be God's next step for us?

You will never be finished with pruning. At every stage of your life, as the time required for a particular responsibility increases, the other things you must prune out to give it the additional time will need to shift. For example, in most cases the most intense time investment in parenting comes in the first four years of life and the four years from age 15 to 19.

Starting a business or new ministry takes a large upfront investment, and other responsibilities will receive less time and energy. When a rocket is launched, the bulk of the fuel is spent lifting it the first few yards off the pad. It is the same with most work: it needs a great deal of momentum to sustain its life. But this season of birthing must not become the normal level of investment, or other roles (such as spouse, parent, or sibling) may lose fruitfulness. Pruning is essential to increasing fruitfulness.[11]

It is only one word, but there is a major shift in perspective when I clarify who I am responsible *for* and who I am responsible *to*. God declares that I am responsible *to* my spouse, my children, my parents and many others. But I am only responsible *for* myself. I cannot cross the line and seek to take over the responsibilities others in my life have *for* their lives. God, who loves the world, does not take over the responsibilities he has assigned to each person.

I am responsible *to* my parents as one of their adult children. My siblings and I may have to make decisions to have them moved from their home into a place of safety and care when they are no longer able to sustain themselves. But I am not responsible *for* their happiness in this transition. They are still responsible *for* their attitude and reactions to this earthquake of change.

A woman with an alcoholic husband is not responsible for him becoming sober and being a good husband. She is responsible *to* him to be a loving wife and but she cannot be responsible *for* his choices about his drinking. That clarification helps her define exactly what her "work" is in that relationship and prunes any attempts to control, fix or change her husband.

Remember the serenity prayer. "God, grant me the serenity to accept the things I cannot change, the courage to change the things I can, and the wisdom to know the difference." There is also a relational version of this prayer. "God grant me the serenity to accept the people I cannot change, the courage to change the one I can, and the wisdom to know it is me."[12]

2.   Consistently use a process to accomplish your defined work.

Defined work is a clear list of actions and projects that we know are part of carrying out our responsibilities. It includes single actions like returning a phone call, making an online purchase, replying to an e-mail, and preparing a message. Many workers have a hundred or more actions scattered on a variety of "to-do" lists for our responsibilities as spouse, parent and employee. We can also identify 30 to 70 projects that are part of our defined work. Leading a small group meeting, planning the coming year of sermons, or hiring a new staff member are all tasks that contain more than one action. They are what time management coach, David Allen, calls "projects".[13]

Effective work, Allen says, requires that we collect, decide, act on, and evaluate all of these actions and projects. Dallas Willard warns against writing "checks" that we cannot cash with our time.[14] We would confront a friend who was mailing out checks with nothing in the account to honor them. Yet many of us, perhaps with an out-of-balance desire to please others, or a confusion of what it means to be a servant leader, make time commitments we really do not have the resources to supply.

Here are some practical steps to managing work and rest:

1.   Start by looking at a year. Divide the twelve months into segments that have some common theme or challenges that will impact your decisions with your time.

Here is an example:

Segment One: mid-August to mid-November. The launch of a school year and often includes several critical annual ministry events. Everything from dance classes to football kicks off.

Segment Two: late November to early January. Thanksgiving, Christmas, and the New Year holidays will influence your calendar and change the rhythm from the fall.

Segment Three: early January to early April. Similar to segment one, it provides opportunity for ministry focus and advance on a weekly basis.

Segment Four: early April to May. Easter, Spring Break, Mother's Day, graduations, and the Memorial Day weekend are special dates that call for adjustment of time commitments.

Segment Five: June to Mid-August. Vacations, school holidays, camps, conferences, weddings and reunions occur. It can be challenging to get your leadership team all at the same place at the same time during these weeks.

2.   Now take each segment and using a 12-month calendar, write in:

Non-negotiable and previous commitments that would be very difficult to change. Include not only work but family and personal commitments. At this point you are not making new commitments. These are settled dates that need to be taken into account before making other additions.

Dedicated time for renewal and quality time with loved ones. If you are married, sit down with your spouse and write in specific dates for the next two segments. If it is March, work on dates for April through mid-August. If a weekend speaking request conflicts with a date my wife and I had planned as a weekend of rest, I have two choices: 1) decline, saying I already have a commitment on that date, or 2) discuss the opportunity with my wife to move our date to a nearby open date and accept the engagement. Notice that simply erasing a date that reflects one of my life's most important relationships is not an option. I know there must be exceptions and there will be sacrifices but I meet many leaders who say "yes" to everyone else and the ones making all of the sacrifices are the ones closest to them. Sometimes what is called sacrifice is really a failure to love those God has given us responsibility to love.

Activities that need a specific date to be determined later. As you look beyond the next two segments of your year, make a list of activities that you know about, but for which the specific dates are not yet set. For example: decisions about travels to visit family at the Christmas holidays, a family wedding that you know will be next June but don't yet have date, an overseas mission trip that is 18 months away but does not have exact dates.

Now go back to the two segments of the year that are coming up next and look at each week. What needs to be included so that you are intentionally pursuing fruitful work? Write in regular commitments like staff meetings that are already anticipated but could be moved to a different day if others involved are notified in advance.

Fear is the opposite of stepping out in faith, but we often dress our fear in nice, easy work that keeps us busy. A mentor can help us see how we can be more effective in investing in fruitful work and not just busy work. What needs to be added, pruned or moved to create time to care for those in your love and care, including yourself? I suggest blocking out one day every three to four months for prayer, fasting and seeking God's wisdom. If you don't commit to them in advance, the urgent needs that come up will usually crowd them out.

It is also possible for good activities like newsletters or message preparation to become smoke that blinds us from investing in fruitful life-on-life ministry. A pastor that I know began to see that the whole church staff had allowed a massive monthly church newsletter (16 pages that probably went unread in most church households) to take up many hours each week that could be better used in direct ministry with people.

Include in your plans time for review and refinement of your time decisions. Each week, spend one to two hours reviewing and planning the coming week (see David Allen's book *Getting Things Done* for some tips). Set aside a few hours in a block during each of your segments of the year to review and adjust dates for the upcoming two segments. For example: Take one day in early May to look carefully at June through August. Discuss options and make decisions for mid-August through mid-November, including updating your list of pending activities. Often taking a few hours at the end of a vacation or rest period is a good time to make wise choices regarding future commitments.

3.   Let "counting the cost" show up on your weekly schedule. A two-hour leadership meeting on Tuesday afternoon takes more than the two hours if it is to be done in a fruitful, productive way. I may need to schedule planning and preparation for the meeting a week before it occurs so I can communicate and delegate to others on the team items needing attention. I will also need to plan some time on Wednesday morning to communicate and implement decisions made during the meeting. In many cases a two-hour leadership meeting may

have an actual "cost" of six to eight hours.

One benefit of scheduling the real cost of meetings was that I reduced the number of meetings by investing more in the ones we had. There was a greater productivity from meetings, which meant fewer were needed. If meetings are a major tool you use to accomplish work, see Patrick Lencioni's *Death By Meeting.*

4.   Don't make a commitment when you are first asked. When someone calls or sends you an e-mail asking for a future commitment, thank them for asking, ask them for the deadline for needing your decision, and commit to a date to letting them know your decision. This gives you the opportunity to look at the true cost of the commitment in light of the several weeks surrounding the request.

5.   Often the best creativity shows up in moments when we are rested and are not directly working on something. Be careful not to abandon rest or pollute your rest with work. Capture the creativity that bubbles to the surface when you are resting. I always carry paper and a pencil with me because during early morning walks or just playing in the dirt of my flower bed suddenly a light bulb of illumination goes off in my head and the solution is just there.

6.   Creativity often also shows up in the face of urgent crisis. Running into a storm of crisis and unplanned disaster can also be the place where "necessity becomes the mother of invention." Often, however, the people best able to create during a crisis are also people who possess strength and vitality built up from periods of rest and stamina over a period of time so they have adequate reserves for the moment of testing.

7.   Ask God for wisdom to practice relational integrity. Recognize that God brings people into your life for what he is doing in their lives, not just helping you accomplish your work. I will never forget a lunch years ago I had with a pastor who served in the same community with me. Ben shared with me how God had convicted him that almost every appointment in his schedule was driven by his agenda. He said, "I set up most of my lunches to challenge someone to consider serving, giving, or helping with a ministry need. I trained, coached, counseled, equipped, and worked on people over breakfast and lunch several times a week—but the subtle goal driving most of those times was

to get *my* goals accomplished." In tears he went on to describe committing a certain number of appointment times each week to just be with people with no agenda except to love them by listening, caring, celebrating, and entering into what God was doing in their lives.

I returned to my office that afternoon and thumbing back through recent weeks in my appointment book saw the same pattern Ben had described. I called one of my core leaders and we made a lunch appointment. As soon as we were seated and finished our usual small talk he looked at me and said, "So, pastor, what can I do for you?" I replied, "Nothing I just wanted to be with you and see what God is really doing in your life." So we talked some more but after we ordered, after the food arrived, and again as we finished eating and they brought coffee, he repeatedly asked what I needed or wanted from him. And each time I mentioned just wanting to enjoy listening and being with a brother in Christ. Suddenly tears came up in the edge of his eyes. He looked at me intently and said, "I have been an elder, treasurer and other leadership roles in this church, and another church, for many years and I have never had a pastor just want to *be* with me." It was a life-changing moment for us both.

It also set me wondering if my appointments with God were out of balance. Was a love relationship being lost in my work-defined focus where my agenda was defining and driving the time? Have you ever had a tire out of balance on your car? It not only rides rough, but it can also be dangerous and it shortens the life of the tire. God made us for work and for rest but really both are simply to be different places for loving God and loving others. Work and rest are not the end goals; they are the means to a loving life.

Healthy life management lets me bring the rhythm of a *time to work* and a *time to rest* into a healthier way of relating. There is nothing wrong with bringing a team together and working hard, but there is a need—perhaps more than many of us realize—to just be with, love, listen, and replenish each other.

Congratulations! You have completed this short study that introduces you to seeing your time as God views it. Now comes the challenging part. Reading about work and rest from God's perspective is easier than choosing it. Share this book with someone you can see on a regular basis and then commit to helping each other live in God's rhythm. Use some of the resources found in the end notes for further reading to address many questions I have not addressed. Unwrap every day as a gift from the God who loves you and purchased a life of joy for you.

Truly, truly, I say to you, you will weep and lament, but the world will rejoice. You will be sorrowful, but your sorrow will turn into joy. When a woman is giving birth, she has sorrow because her hour has come, but when she has delivered the baby, she no longer remembers the anguish, for joy that a human being has been born into the world. So also you have sorrow now, but I will see you again, and your hearts will rejoice, and no one will take your joy from you. In that day you will ask nothing of me. Truly, truly, I say to you, whatever you ask of the Father in my name, he will give it to you. Until now you have asked nothing in my name. Ask, and you will receive, that your joy may be full.

—John 16:20-24 ESV

STUDY GUIDE

STUDY GUIDE

For each chapter of the text you will find the following sections:

EXPLORE

After reading the chapter, these questions and exercises will prompt you to reflect and think more deeply on how this impacts your life. Practice being still and reflecting on God's truth, and remembering God's promises. Take a walk or find some other way to be in alert prayer where your heart comes into alignment with God's heart.

EXPERIENCE

When we read and then translate into practice, it has the potential to produce lasting change and growth. Explore, experiment, try it on, kick the tires. Testing truth to see how it translates into your life is the only way to begin change.

EVALUATE

Discussing what you learned from your experience has a way of influencing others and also drills the lessons deeper into your own life. Asking questions of what went well, what went wrong, and what was meaningful is a sure way to move from just an experience to a shaping or change in lifestyle. We all tend to drift back into old habits, so inviting an outside voice to alert you to blind spots and losing focus can be very helpful.

CHAPTER 1

EXPLORE

A breakthrough for me in addressing my time was to make the connection between time and love. We were created to receive and give love. Time becomes the space where you make the love exchange. What do these passages teach you about being a loving person?

1. Matthew 10:28-31
2. John 12:23-32
3. Romans 5:1-8
4. Romans 8:31-39
5. Galatians 5:5-6

Pray Matthew 6:9-13. Pay special attention to the request for daily bread. Would your inner life of thoughts and attitudes be different if you were trusting God for the essential resources needed to live one day at a time?

Read the rest of Matthew 6. What does Jesus teach about investing our time?

EXPERIENCE

Listen closely to what is going on inside your spirit when you put work on pause. Write in your journal a response to these questions. Are you enjoying unwrapping God's gift of a rest day? When you stop working, are you constantly revving your engine because you see the down time as an attack on your productivity? Does getting things done have a higher value than loving?

Experiment with reflecting on what God is teaching you from your past and then translating those lessons into your present choices.

"Hope is not simply wishful thinking; it is a fruit of the Spirit born of the spiritual discipline of remembering."[15]

Journal, draw a picture, blog—find a way to capture lessons from your past.

Steven Covey writes about "beginning with the end in mind." How is the reality of Christ returning, setting up a kingdom, and your eternal life with him impacting your present choices? Capture your thoughts. Record, write a song, put a saying on the wall in your office.

EVALUATE

With a coach:
1. Describe the specific assistance you need from others to help you with time/life management.
2. Identify one or more people you need to invite to assist you in your time/life management journey. When will you get with them and how will you tap their wisdom or support?
3. Discuss your experiments from the section above in "capturing"lessons from your past and your anticipation of Christ's coming kingdom.
4. Think back over the last several months. Did you invest too much time in attempting to change the past or control the future? How do you know when you're going beyond the responsibility God has given you?
5. Recall moments where you worked or rested well. Can you identify what made those moments good?

CHAPTER 2

EXPLORE

Read 2 Corinthians 1:3–11 and Proverbs 14:29–31. Look for examples of the circles of responsibility and influence. What do these passages say about your responsibility *for* and responsibility **to** influence?

EXPERIENCE

How often do you feel:	Never	Sometimes	Often
1. Tired	N	S	O
2. Anxious	N	S	O
3. Driven	N	S	O
4. Weary	N	S	O
5. Judgmental	N	S	O
6. Bored	N	S	O
7. Touchy	N	S	O
8. Resentful	N	S	O

What patterns do you see in your responses? What choices, beliefs, or expectations feed these symptoms of fatigue?

How would you choose to invest your time differently this week if you tear up your "sacred" and "secular" boxes and instead view every moment as a gift from a loving God?

Honestly examine your prayers. Do you tend to ask God's blessing on *your* work or do you seek his help so you can be a part of *his* work? What difference does it make whose work it is?

Stop at the end of each day for a week and think back over your day. Were there times when you left God out of your day? Did you slip into a mindset that "this is spiritual" o. "this is secular?" How did God give you opportunity to influence others to move closer to Christ?

EVALUATE

With a coach:

1. Do the people who know you best see you as a person ready to give and invest in others, or as exhausted and surviving from one task to the next meeting?
2. What did you learn from your end-of-the-day view of your choices and your view of time?
3. Are you living with intentionality or simply reacting to life like a batter in front of a fast pitching machine?
4. Are you playing "offense" or "defense" in your goals and choices to act?
5. What are examples of recent choices that were motivated by fear?
6. What are some examples of choices based on faith?

CHAPTER 3

EXPLORE

Make a grid of some of the "fields" you are working in right now. Take a life inventory by listing all of your roles and major responsibilities currently included with each role. Here's a sample—make your own in your journal.

Role	Current Responsibilities	Outcome/ "Harvest"	Actions/ "Sowing"
Spouse	Decision on moving	To help my partner reach his/her full potential in Christ	Weekly time to encourage, ask questions and pray together
Parent	Being available and intentional with my adult children	Maintain a safe and supportive space for everyone in the family	Plan time with my son-in-law to really get to know him where he works and plays (go fishing together)
Employee	Publish book on time management; Hire a new team member	Serve a network of pastors and church leaders so they are healthy and effective	Maintain a specific prayer ministry for leaders God brings into my circle
Adult Child	Invite my parents for a visit	To help my parents cope with aging	Take initiative to contact them and send them notes of encouragement
Sibling	Call my brother and sister once a week	Maintain a close caring support for each other	Link up through Skype

Remind yourself of what the "fruit" should be for each role. For example: What should you be "sowing" into your relationship with your spouse to experience a godly harvest? My wife and I commit turning off the TV early enough in the evening to join hands and thank God for the day and to bring the needs of tomorrow to him. This helps us harvest faith anchored to God and not our circumstances.

What stage of the seed-to-fruit cycle best describes the work needed in each of your fields? How does sowing, nurturing, protecting or harvesting apply to each effort?

EXPERIENCE

1. Write out your prayer requests this week. Each day look at a few of your relationships and roles (see list below to get started) and write out a few specific requests for how you need God to bring "fruit" into this area of relationship or responsibility in your life.
   - Spouse
   - Parent
   - Sibling
   - Friend
   - Citizen
   - Church Member
   - Employee
   - Neighbor
   - Other

2. When you look back over what you pray are your requests too small in light of who God is and what He is doing?

EVALUATE

With a coach:

1. Evaluate your list. Are you trying to work in too many different fields? Are you sure you are standing in the fields assigned to you by God? Are you spending too much energy looking at others, judging how they are choosing to labor and telling them how to do it "right?" (Romans 14:4)
2. What resistance are you encountering either from within or from outside attack? God often uses work and the resistance he allows to advance his work in our hearts. He may be transforming a prideful "I can do it myself" attitude into a healthy interdependence of humility. He often uses painful

circumstances to set us free from relying on ourselves and to bring us to a place of relying on him and the contribution of others, especially through their prayers. (2 Corinthians 1:8–11)

3. Do you tend to get angry or be thankful when encountering resistance?

4. Explore some specific ways that resistance in your working duties is changing a prideful heart to a humility that says:

   "I need help!"

   "My resources are not enough."

   "I need God to show up!"[16]

5. How does it change the way you view your schedule if you see "work time" as a more holistic part of your life rather than just your employment?

6. How can you aim at fruitfulness in all of your assigned roles?

7. How can you walk a balance between expecting resistance but not falling into despair or cynicism?

CHAPTER 4

EXPLORE

What do these passages teach about practices of working and resting?

1. 1 Timothy 6:19
2. Acts 20:17–38
3. Psalm 28:4–9
4. Philippians 3:7–14
5. Psalm 128
6. Matthew 6:19–34

EXPERIENCE

1. Is there a hobby or pleasurable activity that is gathering dust because you have neglected it?
2. Journal about how it nourishes you and increases your joy and vitality.
3. Practice a 24-hour Sabbath and then write down in your journal what God is teaching you from the experience.

EVALUATE

1. Why do you think our culture fails to rest in a renewing way?
2. How does our cultural view of rest differ from the biblical view?
3. What hindrances to renewing rest do you encounter on a regular basis?
4. What would it look like to find a way around them?
5. Do you believe that God supplies all you need to obey any command he gives you?
6. What has God given you to help you rest every seventh day?

CHAPTER 5

EXPLORE

One of the key ideas in this chapter was the practice of relational integrity. Reflect on these two passages: 1 Corinthians 13, 1 Peter 4:7–11. How can you detect your real motivation and agenda as you approach time with a person?

EXPERIENCE

Look back over all five lessons. List three to five specific actions you will take to improve your life management. Now develop a plan for how the next year will have a different rhythm for you.

EVALUATE

1. How would you contrast a cultural management of time with a biblical perspective?
2. What are your goals for the next six months in the following areas:
   a. Physical
   b. Mental
   c. Emotional
   d. Social
   e. Spiritual
3. Even though the five coaching sessions are at an end, discuss what kind of support and accountability would help you to live out a biblical plan for your time.
4. What has worked or not worked?
5. How can you actually make a consistent lifestyle change?

NOTES

[1] 2 Corinthians 12: 1-10

[2] Theologians call this "general revelation" because it can be learned by any observer of the world around us.

[3] Theologians call this "special revelation." By this they mean that this level of understanding the mind and heart of God cannot be figured out by us. We are dependent of God to pull back the curtain and show us this truth. The Bible is the source of special revelation.

[4] Job 1:21

[5] Ecclesiastes 3:11

[6] 1 Corinthians 11:24

[7] Mark Buchanan. *The Rest of God: Restoring Your Soul by Restoring Sabbath.* Nashville: W Publishing, 2006. Page 196.

[8] J. Grant Howard. *Balancing Life's Demands: A New Perspective on Priorities.* Sisters, OR: Multonomah, 1994. A good study calling us to examine our roles from a biblical perspective.

[9] Jim Loen & Tony Schwartz. *The Power of Full Engagement: Managing Energy, Not Time, is the Key to High Performance & Personal Renewal.* New York: Free Press, 2003. Page 13.

[10] Pete Scazzero is pastor of New Life Fellowship and author of two excellent books *The Emotionally Healthy Church* and *Emotionally Healthy Spirituality* (purchase the books and other resources at: www.emotionallyhealthy.org). Pete's sermon series on Sabbath is excellent. New Life Fellowship is really working out the joy of being a healthy, multi-ethnic community of Christ-followers.

[11] A helpful resource in deciding what is important is found in *The Seven Habits of Highly Effective People* by Stephen Covey. The entire book relates to these lessons but his explanation of the Four Quadrants of Urgency and Importance are an essential perspective.

[12] John G. Miller. *QBQ! The Question Behind the Question.* New York: G.P. Putnam, 2004. Page 79.

[13] The best resource I have found for sharpening and implementing these skills is *Getting Things Done* by David Allen (for more information visit: www.davidco.com).

14 I was a student under Dallas Willard during my D.Min studies at Fuller Theological Seminary. This is a paraphrase from one of his lectures.

15 Gary Haugen. *Just Courage: God's Great Expedition for the Restless Christian.* Downers Grove, IL: InterVarsity Press, 2008.

16 In our work as parents, Pandora and I have come into each new stage of parenting praying something like this, "Lord, we have never parented (teenagers, young adults, or married children) before. This is a new work for us. We sense our great need for you to provide us with the daily bread we are going to need to do this work well." It is God's intent that our work, in the various roles he has given to us, takes us to a place of repentance from relying on ourselves and discovering the abundant life that comes as we are dependent on him and interdependent with others. We pray that God will bring other people into the lives of our children to meet needs we cannot meet. And we have a long list of thanksgiving for small group leaders, friends and "adopted grandparents" who have ministered to our children. We do not walk alone!

Made in the USA
Lexington, KY
16 January 2013